the little
book of **peace**

SUSAN JEFFERS, PH.D.

the little
book of **peace**

The bestselling author of
End the Struggle and Dance with Life

Hodder & Stoughton

First published in Great Britain in 2001 by Hodder and Stoughton
A division of Hodder Headline

2   4   6   8   10   9   7   5   3   1

A CIP catalogue record for this title is available from the British Library

ISBN 0 340 81823 9

Printed and bound in Great Britain by
Omnia Books Limited, Glasgow

Hodder and Stoughton
A division of Hodder Headline
338 Euston Road
London NW1 3BH

Do the work
Let go of the fight
Embrace the flow
Aah, peace...

SJ

CONTENTS

introduction

ALL IS WELL!

Peace of mind...where does it come from? It is clear to me that those who approach life with serenity rather than struggle have discovered the secret of 'dancing with life'. They have learned how to move into the flow of their experiences—good or bad—with a feeling of harmony, trust, gratitude, and love. They have found a way of convincing their frightened minds that 'ALL IS WELL'. The good news is that we can all learn how to dance with life as well.

Throughout this little book, you will find
in capsule form many of the calming
thoughts found in 'End the Struggle and
Dance with Life'. I encourage you to read
it over and over and over again. And
when the weight of the world seems to
be getting you down, open it to any page
to help lighten your spirits. In time, the
healing messages within will teach you
the real meaning of a peaceful mind.

I've come a long way on this issue of
creating a peaceful mind and I'm amazed
at how obvious are the causes of our
upsets in life, big or small. I'm reminded

of the ancient saying, 'The road is smooth. Why do you throw rocks before you?' We all throw rocks before us, sometimes making our Journey very difficult. So let's begin clearing the debris to make way for a more joyful, abundant...and peaceful...life!

Susan Jeffers, May 2001

rIsIng
above the **clouds**

SOMETHING WONDROUS
IN YOUR BEING

I have a wonderful statue of the
Laughing Buddha. He is always there to
remind me that true joy comes not from
something out there, but from something
wondrous within our being. This
'something wondrous' is ever-present and
always accessible. As a result, we all have
the ability to reach this place of peace
within where we can feel safe, abundant
and truly able to dance with life.

IT'S THERE
FOR THE TAKING

I call the wondrous place within our
being the Higher Self. When we 'live in'
the realm of the Higher Self, we
experience all the divine qualities such as
caring, joy, strength, appreciation, and
love. We are free to enjoy the best that
life has to offer. Peace and laughter fill
our hearts.

'HIGHER' IS BETTER!

The Higher Self is the Spiritual part of who we are. Most of us live in the Lower Self. This is the place of struggle, lack, fear, and pain. The good news is that we can begin the Journey toward that place of inner peace right now, right where we are, and with the tools that are presently in our grasp.

THERE IS POWER IN
THE HIGHER SELF

The Higher Self knows we have the strength to handle anything that can ever happen to us. It doesn't see the outside world as a threat; it sees it as a place to learn and grow and contribute. The Higher Self knows that all situations in our life—good or bad—can be used as a teaching for our highest good.

TUNE IN TO THE WISDOM WITHIN

Our Higher Self holds wisdom beyond
our wildest dreams. This incredible
wisdom can lead us to exactly where we
need to go for our highest good. If we
listen, this is what we hear:

'It's all happening perfectly. Whatever happens in my life, I'll handle it. I'll learn from it. I'll make it a triumph!'

THE WORLD IS HUGE WITH POSSIBILITY!

When the Journey inward to the Higher
Self begins, life expands to encompass a
world that is HUGE with possibility.
Bringing a Spiritual dimension into all
that we do is essential for ending the
struggle and dancing with life. Our
bodies and our minds can take us only
so far. Our Spirit can lead us all the way
home.

THE HIGHER SELF IS
THE KEY TO FREEDOM

If you never rise above the level of the
Lower Self, you will never feel free. If
you transcend to the Higher Self, you
will always feel free—despite what is
happening in the outside world! Your
inner peace has nothing to do with the
dramas of your life. (What a relief!)
When you find your way to your Higher
Self, the Laughing Buddha inside of you
will truly begin to laugh!

release

LETTING GO OF HOLDING ON

Most of us don't know how to let go. In
fact, we wear life like a girdle—tight,
hard, rigid, uncomfortable, and
constricting. Oh, how we long to take off
that girdle and breathe deeply and freely!
Oh how we long to let go of all those
things that keep us immersed in struggle
instead of flying above the clouds! Yes,
it's definitely time to let go!

IT FEELS GOOD TO LOOSEN UP

I love the image of 'wearing the world as a loose garment means'. This means: 1) not hanging on so tightly to the way it's supposed to be; 2) trusting that all is well...that life is happening perfectly; 3) seeing the possibility of love and growth that exists in all experiences—good and bad; 4) recognizing that we can face the ebb and flow of life from a place of harmony and peace instead of struggle.

DANCE WITH LIFE

How can we ever learn to dance with life
when we are uptight? Dancing with life
by definition means curving, blending,
bending, circling and flowing—like
nature. 'Bad' dancers are straight, stiff
and methodical, totally out of harmony
with the ceaseless flow of the energy of
the Universe.

GO AROUND THE OBSTACLES

We can learn a lot by watching how water relates to the world around it. It's fluid. It goes around any obstacle in its way. (It doesn't stop to argue!) It flows downstream rather than struggling to push upstream as many of us are doing in life. It just goes with the flow. Perhaps that's why watching the action and rhythm of water is so peaceful to the human psyche.

GO WITH THE FLOW

We weren't born to hold onto positions.
We are meant to flow in a world that is
constantly moving beneath our feet. Say
to yourself:

I am free. I am fluid. I am rich. I am whole. I embrace it all. I am nourished. I have much to give. I can soar. I am at peace. I let go.

UN-SET YOUR HEART

Setting your heart on something is
entering into a state of rigidity. Un-
setting your heart is entering a state of
flow. Set as many goals as you want.
Picture exactly what you would like to
happen. With loving effort, do the
necessary work. And when you are
satisfied that you have done as much as
you can, LET GO OF THE OUTCOME.

IT'S ALL ALRIGHT!

Think about the many little things that cause upset in your life. Forgetting to buy something at the market. Sitting in the airport for hours because the plane was delayed. Rain when you have invited people over for a picnic. It's at these times that we really need to ask ourselves a very profound question: *What if this was all alright?* Instant peace!

SAYING 'YES' FEELS SO GOOD

Saying YES reduces upset and anxiety
and lets you become the creator of
enriching new life experiences. Saying
YES doesn't mean giving up. It means
getting up and acting on your belief that
you can create meaning and purpose in
whatever life hands you. It means
moving into the realm of action. Here
you are able to:

Find the blessing. Find the lesson to be learned. Find the strength you never thought you had. Find the triumph.

Saying YES is a very powerful tool indeed!

DECIDE TO SAY 'YES'

Decide that you have the power to say
YES to it all. Your saying YES guarantees
that you will find the limitless source of
inner strength that lies within. There is
no greater comfort than that. When we
achieve that state of comfort, we can let
go of our need to control not only the
little things, but even the big things in
our lives.

CUT THE CORD

We can't control the behaviour of others.
We must let go and let people in our
lives follow their own path. Co-
dependency is an inability to establish
healthy boundaries between ourselves
and others. As a result, their behaviour
determines our self-esteem, happiness,
and sense of peace and flow. When we
cut the cord, we are free...and so are
they. Hallelujah!

CREATE YOUR OWN HAPPINESS

There is no peace when we depend on other people to fill us up. It feels so much better when we fill ourselves up. If peace in your heart is dependent on how other people are going to act, you are living in the realm of the Lower Self and you will constantly be in conflict. As you cut the cord, you are free to live in the realm of the Higher Self where happiness reigns.

SIMPLICITY BRINGS CALM

Anything that takes away our lightness-
in-living definitely weighs us down. It is
wise to lighten the load—in all areas of
your life. You can't end the struggle
when you are carrying so much weight
within and around you. The trick is to
release that which weighs you down and
embrace that which makes you soar. Are
you flying yet?

LET GO OF EXCESS BAGGAGE

Use and enjoy that which enriches your
life and let the rest go. Start with
cleaning your closets. 'Susan, why, in the
grand scope of life, is cleaning our
closets so important?' Because it creates a
'trickle-down' of relief: As you get rid of
the clutter in your closet, you begin to
realize you don't need (or want!) as
much as you thought you did. What a
relief!

WHAT 'DON'T' YOU NEED?

When you clean your closets, you realize
you don't need to buy as many things,
which means...You don't need as much
space, which means...You don't need to
have a bigger house, which means...
You don't need to earn as much, which
means ...You don't need to work so
hard, which means...You have more
time and energy, which means...
PEACE AT LAST!

THERE IS ALWAYS MORE

You never have to hold onto anything.
You can love it all, enjoy it all, but you
need not hang on. *There is always more.*
As you let go of all the fear and suffering
that attachment brings, you are free. Feel
the relief this freedom brings. Feel
yourself lighten as you let go of all the
unnecessary burdens you have created
for yourself.

seeing with **new** eyes

THE TIME IS 'NOW'

It is time to focus on the miracle of NOW. Most of us are focused on the future. We are constantly waiting for the big moment when our goals, dreams, and desires will be fulfilled. That guarantees us a life of wishing, wanting, and lack of fulfilment. It doesn't have to be that way. We can focus on the gifts and richness of the NOW!

LET GO OF 'GETTING THERE'

Peace comes from knowing we have so
much right now...family, friends, career,
opportunities for contribution and
personal growth, and more. With this
knowledge, we realize that we are not
simply machines trying to reach a
destination. We are hearts and souls
vibrantly connected to everyone and
everything around us each moment of
each day!

THE GIFT OF THE PRESENT

We are told that first we sow the seeds
and later we harvest. In truth, we don't
have to wait for later. When we focus on
the beauty of the now, each moment can
be exquisite. When we focus on the
beauty of the now, we are filled with a
sense of gratitude. When we focus on
the beauty of the now, we are able to
harvest WHILE we are sowing the seeds!

IT'S ALL A MATTER OF
PERCEPTION

If you see your tasks in life as drudgery,
then they are drudgery. On the other
hand, if you see them as a gift of the
Universe coming through you, then your
tasks are done in the spirit of love and
generosity. What a difference your
perception makes!

CLIMB OFF THE LADDER TO DISTRESS

Success is not about goals. Success is
about living a full and balanced life in
partnership with others to create a joyful
feeling of love, contribution, appreciation
and abundance...*despite how our
endeavours may turn out.*

FORGET ABOUT THE GOAL!

We can't learn the art of letting go when
one eye is on the goal. Nor can we learn
the art of embracing all that is beautiful
when one eye is on the goal. That's just
the way it is. We must keep both eyes
on the enjoyment of the process and
forget about the goal!

IF WE LEARN AND GROW FROM OUR MISTAKES, THEN THEY AREN'T MISTAKES.

IF YOU HAVEN'T MADE ANY MISTAKES LATELY, YOU MUST BE DOING SOMETHING WRONG!

WE ARE ALL 'GOOD ENOUGH'

Human beings were not born to be
perfect. We were born to learn, to grow,
to expand, to love, to create, to enjoy,
and to see the beauty in all things—
including ourselves. Our striving for
perfection is a futile endeavour, a waste
of time. Even the most enlightened of us
regularly trip and fall. No one is
perfect... *even the Buddhas have their days!*

ENJOY!

Feelings of accomplishment and
satisfaction do not come from striving to
be perfect. They do come from the
process of using our inner power, beauty
and love in a creative, expansive, positive
and loving way. It doesn't get any better
than that.

ENOUGH IS TRULY ENOUGH!

The word 'ENOUGH' can overcome the
hunger of our MORE–BETTER–BEST
society. ENOUGH implies a sense of
fullness. When we say 'I've had enough'
at the end of a delicious meal, it means
we are full and satisfied. We are not
looking for more. When we include
thoughts of ENOUGH in the deepest
recesses of our being, we can begin to
relax and smell the proverbial roses.

A NEW KIND OF EXCELLENCE

Competition as we know it today is crazy-making and demoralizing. There is a wonderful alternative. We can achieve excellence by acting on our understanding that we have a higher meaning and purpose in this world in whatever form that takes. When we connect with that sense of higher meaning and purpose, our 'performance' is without equal.

EVERYONE HAS THEIR
OWN DANCE TO DANCE

Some of us want to spread our arms
wide to new adventures. Some of us
want to open the curtain just a little bit
for the time being. Some of us want to
light a huge bonfire. Some of us want
just a little flame to radiate our own
special light into the world. Never worry
if you are doing it 'wrong'. There is no
wrong. It's your dance. Every day it's a
new dance for all of us. Trust your own
rhythm. It suits you.

SAY YES TO SAYING NO!

Saying NO is not always a negative.
When we say NO to tasks that
overburden us and take away our peace
of mind, it is a positive. In the
beginning, saying NO can bring on great
anxiety. That's okay! FEEL THE FEAR
AND SAY NO ANYWAY! As you break
the self-destructive habit of taking on
more than you can comfortably handle,
your body and your mind will breathe a
sigh of relief!

43

FOLLOW YOUR HEART

Shoulds and shouldn'ts are signs of our
need to conform. They come from the
Lower Self. They make us worry. They
make us do too much, think too much,
plan too much. They make us loose sight
of who we really are. Remember that
from a Higher-Self perspective, our
enjoyment and contribution to life come
from following our own heart...and
everyone's heart is different.

BE YOUR OWN PERSON

Tune into the wisdom within. The
Higher Self holds wisdom beyond our
wildest dreams that can lead us to
exactly where we need to go for our
highest good. Simply ask your Higher
Self what is right for you to do relative
to your purpose here on earth, listen for
the loving response, then act accordingly.
This is being your own person. This is
being the best that you can be.

BALANCE IS BEAUTIFUL

A balanced life is a gift we can give
ourselves. A balanced life is one that is
filled with the riches of play, intimacy
with family and friends, work, alone
time, and personal growth and more.
When we feel abundant, our addiction to
work falls by the wayside, which is
where it belongs!

TAKE CHARGE OF YOUR LIFE

For peace of mind, it is essential that we
learn to let go of the victim mentality.
The truth is that we are not helpless and
weak. All things in our lives can be used
to empower us, no matter how difficult
they are at the time. Instead of blaming
others, we need to learn how to take
charge of our lives, honour who we are,
and create powerful and beautiful lives
for ourselves.

SAY 'NO' TO BLAME…
'YES' TO PERSONAL POWER!

Any time we blame anyone or anything
for what is happening in our lives, we
are giving away all our power and our
peace of mind. If there is a hell on earth,
living as a victim with feelings of anger
and blame defines it. If there is a heaven
on earth, living powerfully and lovingly
as the creator of our own lives defines it.

TRUST THE UNIVERSE

It is obvious that peace cannot exist
within our hearts with the presence of
fear. I have the perfect antidote:
Whenever fear enters your being, simply
look up and say:

'Okay, Universe. Take over, please. Take
me where you wish. I'll enjoy the ride'.

And then find ways of enjoying the ride.
Perfect!

FIND THE GIFT
IN ALL THINGS

No matter how difficult life may seem,
we can find meaning and purpose in it
all. We can learn and grow from even
the most challenging situations in our
lives. As we learn we can handle it all in
a powerful and loving way, our
confidence grows and grows and grows.
In that lies the gift.

THE TEARS OF 'YES'

It feels so good to enter the Land of Tears. What a merciful relief not to have to hold back that raging river of emotion! The tears of 'YES' remind us that we are part of the human race. They teach us to have compassion for others as we remember that deep within them exists their own Land of Tears, no matter how they may appear on the outside. The tears of 'YES' can be such a gift.

WHEN OPPOSITES GO TOGETHER

Joy and sorrow flow together, the one
embracing the other. Just as we can flow
in the peace of happy experiences, we
can flow in the pain of unhappy
experiences. It helps to see it all as just
part of the richness of life.

WE ARE IN CONTROL

While we can't really ever control
anything 'out there', we can learn to
control the most important thing...our
REACTION to whatever life hands us.
When we are in control of our reactions,
we can be battered by the world around
us and still maintain a wonderful sense
of inner peace.

FIND PEACE
IN THE MYSTERY

Tranquillity comes when we stop asking
'WHY?' I've often been asked: 'Why is
there so much suffering in the world?' If
this question weighs heavily on your
mind, I suggest you stop driving yourself
crazy by expecting an answer that we
ordinary mortals can't provide. Instead,
when the question comes up, tell yourself the following:

'I can't see the Grand Design, the Divine plan for this Universe. Therefore, I no longer will ask why. Instead, I will learn to be more trusting. Life includes suffering. And it is up to me to find a way to be more peaceful and compassionate in the midst of the suffering.'

WE DON'T KNOW
THE 'GRAND DESIGN'

When we let go of our expectations, we
can allow ourselves the peaceful thought
that it's all happening perfectly, no
matter how it turns out. The truth is
that blessings surround us all the time.
We need to focus on the blessings.
That shift in focus isn't a delusion.
In fact: We are deluding ourselves when
we focus on the bad!

WE CAN HANDLE IT ALL!

Yes, life is filled with surprises, some good and some bad. But with the inner knowing that we can handle anything life hands us, we don't have to worry about the future any longer. We can get on with our life with a feeling of freedom and adventure. We can even begin to enjoy the mysteries, instead of feeling threatened by them. It doesn't get any better than that!

find your **centre**

ACQUIRE 'SEA LEGS'

Acquiring sea legs is about letting go of
our resistance and going with the
movement below our feet. In so doing
we can create an incredible sense of flow.
When we have our sea legs, we can
maintain a peaceful state of mind in the
middle of all life's difficulties. By simply
shifting our relationship to all that is
around us, we are able to turn misery
into ecstasy. Heaven!

IT'S ALL ALRIGHT!

Finding our sea legs is a form of centring. When we are centred, we are not affected by externals. Therefore, it doesn't matter what table we get, how heavy the traffic is, how the stock market rises and falls, and so on. Nothing to get. Nothing to change. It's truly all alright!

KEEPING OUR BALANCE

If we leave our centre and are
continually reaching out to others to
satisfy some lack within our selves, we
topple forward. If we constantly
withdraw because of fear, we topple
backward in a state of rigidity. We need
to always come back to centre.

CENTRING BRINGS US SERENITY

When we learn how to centre ourselves, we are not affected as much by the ebb and flow of life. Our fear diminishes greatly. When things are not going according to plan in our outer life, we are positioned well *internally* to weather the storm.

NOTHING 'OUT THERE'
CAN FILL US UP

When we are constantly focused on
externals, we are not centred, that is, we
are not aligned internally—body, mind
and Higher Self. Without that alignment,
we have a case of Divine Homesickness.
We feel empty and lost, always trying to
find our way Home...always looking for
something 'out there' to fill us up. And
nothing out there can.

AWAKEN THE INTUITION

A centred state is one of immense clarity
and focus. As a result, our awareness is
heightened and our intuition is sharp.
When centred, you can 'listen to' and
'feel' the environment in and around
you. In this heightened state of
awareness, you somehow 'know' where
to go, what to do, what to say, and to
whom. Our intuition can always show us
the way.

'GOOD' FRIENDS HELP

Develop friendships with positive people
rather than 'complaint buddies'. People
who are always complaining are not
centred; by definition, they are letting
the world around them affect their
happiness . . . and ours, if we allow it!
When we are choosing 'centred' friends,
we are creating a more stable
environment for ourselves.

REACH OUT WITH CONFIDENCE AND LOVE

When entering a room, stand tall as if you were powerful and loving; affirm that no matter what reaction you get, you are a worthwhile person who has much to give to this world; focus on what you are going to give rather what you are going to get in the way of approval or acceptance from other people; radiate your loving energy from your centre to everyone around you.

SPREAD YOUR LOVE AROUND

Don't hold back. Give the gift of who
you are to everyone around you. Make
your essence warm this world as far as
the eye can see. Visualize those who
receive your powerful spark of life being
nourished by your gift. Feel the
incredible beauty of just being alive.

embracing

EXQUISITE MOMENTS

When I was a little girl, my father used
to tell me that 'life is a mass of boredom,
interjected with a few exquisite
moments'. And for many years, I
believed him. But not anymore. I wish
he were still alive so that I could tell him
that he was mistaken…that life can be a
mass of exquisite moments interjected
with a few moments of boredom!

LIFE IS HUGE!
LIFE IS TO BE EMBRACED!

OPEN YOUR EYES

As you open your eyes to the wonder around you, you will find that any of the boredom in your life will immediately be replaced by exquisite moments. Your joy, your happiness, your satisfaction and your ability to dance with life depend solely on what you pay attention to. Thankfully, what you pay attention to is entirely up to you!

DON'T TAKE THINGS FOR GRANTED

Taking things for granted is one of the greatest assaults on the quality of our lives. When we take things for granted, we never get to see the magnitude of the gifts that are constantly being placed before us. As a result, we feel only scarcity instead of abundance. The truth is *there is so much to be grateful for that it staggers the imagination!*

MAKE THE ORDINARY
EXTRAORDINARY

We need to see things anew. We need to make the ordinary in our life extraordinary. When we do this, things may remain the same on the outside, but internally, a gentle revolution is taking place. Little by little, we begin to replace the struggle in our lives with a sense of abundant flow.

LOOK MINDFULLY...
LOOK DEEPLY

We can embrace the gifts of magic and
excitement in the most ordinary of
events—eating breakfast, balancing our
cheque-book, getting our cars washed,
driving to work, caring for a loved one,
working, brushing our teeth, and so on.
The trick is to learn how to live in the
moment, paying attention to the wonder
of it all.

LOOK DEEPLY

Most of us only skim the surface when
we look at what life gives to us. This is
why we habitually take things for
granted and miss the miracle of it all. As
we look deeply, we see that in everything
we do, we have been handed the
Kingdom. May we always remember this.

SAY 'THANK YOU' FOR
ALL YOUR GIFTS

The inclusion of the words THANK YOU
in our vocabulary sets up an interesting
paradox. Each time we say these two
powerful words, we are acknowledging a
gift we are given. By definition, if we say
THANK YOU often enough, any trace of
a poverty consciousness disappears; we
begin feeling incredibly abundant!

GIVING FEELS GREAT

Giving is an important part of embracing our abundance. Make it a daily ritual to include one pay-back item on your daily to-do list—whether it's contributing time or money to one of your favourite charities, sending a thank you note, buying a gift for someone, or whatever it is for you. No question about it! Giving feels great!

GIVING COMES FROM
THE BEST OF WHO WE ARE

Giving is Higher Self behaviour. As we
become a giver, we lose our temper less,
we care more about the state of the
environment, we don't need as much as
we thought we did, we are kinder to
others. Giving has many ripple effects in
making ours an incredibly wonderful
world.

**DON'T MISS OUT ON ANOTHER
MOMENT OF GREATNESS IN YOUR
LIFE. YOUR WORLD IS RICH.
HARVEST THE RICHES NOW!**

listen
to the **silence**

QUIET THE MIND

Whatever the method, the purpose of
quieting the mind is always the same—
to step out of our own way and touch a
Universal oneness with all things.

LISTEN TO THE SILENCE

In order to fully embrace the riches in
our lives, we need to go deep within our
being and listen to the important
messages we hold inside. In order to do
this, we must learn how to embrace the
silence, how to quiet the endless chatter
of the Lower Self, so that we can hear
the wisdom of the Higher Self.

A QUIET MIND IS
A PEACEFUL MIND

One way to quiet the mind is through meditation. In meditation, we watch our thoughts passing by as if they were clouds on a sunny day. We learn that thoughts are just thoughts, and we don't have to get attached to the drama they can bring. In thinking this way, we stop our thoughts from driving us crazy.
Peace at last!

WAIT FOR THE ANSWER

When something is deeply troubling
you, just sit with it. Don't DO anything.
Listen to the wisdom within your being.
Eventually you will get the answers you
are seeking. In the emptiness, all things
fall into place. It is a strange paradox
that in emptying the mind, we find
exquisite fullness.

SILENCE IS THE MUSIC OF SERENITY

As we turn off the sound and move into silence, the dancing can begin. We finally hear the music of our Soul, and it is this that gives us peace. And as we listen to the music of our Soul, we mysteriously and wondrously hear the music of everyone else's as well…and we are at one with the world.

TALK TO THE 'CHIEF'

Prayer can bring peace to a struggling
mind...even if you don't believe in God!
But it has to be the right kind of prayer.
Prayers that ask for something set us up
for an immense amount of
disappointment. Sometimes they are
answered and sometimes they're not. It's
all up to the Grand Design; it's not up to
us. We must learn to trust that it's all
happening perfectly!

A PRAYER THAT
BRINGS US PEACE

The following prayer never disappoints.
It is a prayer of trust and appreciation.
Take this prayer into your heart and
notice the struggle abating and the peace
radiating throughout your being:

'I trust that no matter what happens in my life, it is for my highest good. And no matter what happens in the lives of those I love, it is for their highest good. From all things put before us, we shall become stronger and more loving people. I am grateful for all the beauty and opportunity you put into my life. And in all that I do, I shall seek to be a channel for your love.'

PEACE AT LAST!

When we pray regularly, using prayers of
trust and appreciation, the benefits spill
over into all areas of our lives. We come
to realise that the Universal Light is with
us at all times. We need only to tap into
it to find an exquisite piece of 'Heaven'
that we can take into our hearts and
radiate out to everyone whose lives
touches ours. In this place, our fear
disappears and is replaced by an intense
sense of love and caring. Yes, peace
at last!

lighten up

**SET YOUR DIAL TO HAPPINESS!
YOU OWE IT TO YOURSELF TO
LAUGH MORE, PLAY MORE, AND
FULLY EMBRACE THE
EXPERIENCE OF LIFE!**

SMILE...A LOT!

We can begin the process of lightening up and bringing joy into our lives with a simple smile. Smile when you are feeling troubled. Smile as you walk down the street. Smile when you awaken each morning. Smile when you look in that mirror. How does it feel? Lighter? Happier? Oh, yes!

MASTER THE BELLY LAUGH!

It's easy to create a smile but much
harder to create a laugh. But create it we
must! Why? Laughter is very healthy. It
changes our internal chemistry from
negative to positive. Laughter gives us an
internal massage, reaching many organs
of the body. Laughter is an amazing
exercise. And the good news is that it
tightens the belly.

LAUGH A LOT!

Laughter releases tension.
Laughter makes life wonderful.
Laughter balances the heavy with
lightness.
Laughter is contagious.
Laughter brightens up the world!

all in its
own **time**

ALLOW THE MOMENTS OF CONFUSION

Upset in your life is not a sign that something has gone wrong, only that something is changing. Change usually brings confusion. But one day we 'live into' clarity once again, at least for a while. Confusion and clarity, confusion and clarity, confusion and clarity seem to be the rhythm of growth.

GROWTH HAS ITS OWN PACE

We live in an instant world where
everything has speeded up beyond our
grasp. But we are not instant people, and
that is where much of the confusion lies.
Yes, there are many things that can be
done speedily, but when it comes to
Spiritual growth, the pace is slow. That's
just the way it is.

SPIRITUAL GROWTH IS
NEVER-ENDING

Never-ending means that there is always
much more to learn; you never 'get
there'. Spiritual growth is not a
destination. It is a forever process of
expanding and exploring and
discovering. Therefore, when you focus
on the goal, your attention is misplaced.
Pay attention to what you need to learn
right here and right now.

WHEN WE THINK NOTHING IS HAPPENING...IT IS

There is always an unseen world of energy moving and changing within and around us. TRUST is the essential ingredient for feeling peaceful while these unseen forces do their work.

WHEN WE ARE IMPATIENT, IT MEANS WE HAVE NO TRUST

Everything happens in its own perfect time. From nature we learn to have patience by simply watching how seeds hidden beneath the earth slowly emerge to create bowers of beauty. We learn the concept of 'this too shall pass' by watching storms turn into sunshine. We learn about ups and downs by watching the rhythms, the cycles, the ebb and flow, the harmony and the interplay of all things.

LIFE IS AN EXCITING ADVENTURE

If we have the patience to sit there with
the attitude of 'Aha! I wonder what this
experience is going to teach me' then we
can live more with a spirit of mystery
and adventure rather than with a feeling
of fear and helplessness and impatience.

Life IS truly exciting!

CHANGE IS THE ONLY CONSTANT

Ultimately, we learn that there are no
shortcuts. The process is the process and
there's not much we can do about it. We
all want the quick and easy, but when it
comes to becoming a Spiritual being,
speed doesn't work. We are going for a
deep change in the depth of our being.
This is a lifetime process.

SLOW AND STEADY WINS THE RACE

In a world of deadlines and stress it is wonderful to know that there is one area in our life where it is better not to rush, and that is the area of Spiritual growth.

TIME IS ON YOUR SIDE

When you stop thinking that you have
to do it all now, your impatience
dissolves into the sweet flow that is the
natural rhythm of life. And as you
continue your step-by-step journey,
inward and upward to the best of who
you are, life just gets better and better
and better and better.

PEACE IS ABOUT...

releasing, embracing, meditating, being
joyful, being peaceful, being mindful,
being balanced, creating rituals, giving
thanks, slowing down, centring, knowing
that all is well, transcending the petty,
climbing the ladder to true success,
feeling safe, having patience, flowing
with the Universe.

IT'S ALL WITHIN YOU

You have the power to create more and more exquisite moments in your life. These exquisite moments come with the creation of an inner trust...trust in the process, trust in yourself, and trust in the Divine Mystery of it all.

YOU DESERVE THE BEST THAT
LIFE HAS TO OFFER. AND IT'S
REASSURING TO KNOW THAT
YOU DON'T HAVE TO GO
OUTSIDE YOURSELF TO FIND THE
BEST; IT LIES WITHIN YOUR VERY
BEING:

The best lies within your Higher Self, the part of you that sees everything that is a glorious adventure, the part of you that embraces the abundance of gifts that are placed before you, the part of you that notices and is grateful for the miracle of it all, the part of you that knows that you are a vibrantly meaningful part of the Grand Design.

YOU'RE ON THE RIGHT PATH

The most important thing you can do for
yourself is to follow the Path that takes
you to the best of who you are. Finding
the enormous amount of power and love
that lies within is the secret to ending
the struggle and dancing with life. So
COMMIT to this wonderful Journey of
self-discovery!

COMMITMENT IS POWERFUL

Commitment creates a radiant energy
that activates all sorts of 'miracles'. I've
seen these miracles in my life, and you
will see them in yours. Trust me when I
tell you that there is NOTHING that can
stop you once you make that
commitment to create a life of trust,
peace, beauty, lightness, abundance, love
and joy!

EMBRACE THE JOURNEY...
EMBRACE WHO YOU ARE...
EMBRACE ALL THERE IS...

nothing can
stop you **now!**